EXILES OF DESIRE

EXILES OF DESIRE

juan felipe herrera
Arte Publico Press, Houston

ISBN 0-934770-50-6

Cover Photography: Yolanda M. Lopez
Cover Design: Rupert Garcia
Text Layout and Design: Cecilia Brunazzi

Arte Publico Press
University of Houston
University Park
Houston, Texas 77004

For Chente Quintana

ACKNOWLEDGMENTS

I am grateful to the following publications for printing various poems in this volume: *Alcatraz 2*, *Cenizas*, *The Denver Quarterly*, *El Tecolote Literario*, *Metamorfosis*, *Obligatory Hug*, *Oboe 6*, *Red Trapeze*, *Revista Chicano-Riqueña*, *The Threepenny Review* and *Vórtice*.

Part of this manuscript was written during the period of the National Endowment for the Arts Writer's Fellowship 1980.

Ode to the Industrial Village of the World is dedicated to El Teatro de La Esperanza and Sally Barros.

TABLE OF CONTENTS

EXILES OF DESIRE

EXILES

and I heard an unending scream piercing nature.
—from the diary of Edvard Munch/1892

At the greyhound bus stations, at airports, at silent wharfs
the bodies exit the crafts. Women, men, children; cast out
from the new paradise.

They are not there in the homeland, in Argentina, not there
in Santiago, Chile; never there no more in Montevideo, Uruguay
and they are not here

in *America*

They are in exile: a slow scream across a yellow bridge
the jaws stretched, widening, the eyes multiplied into blood
orbits, torn, whirling, spilling between two slopes; the sea, black,
swallowing all prayers, shadeless. Only tall faceless figures
of pain flutter across the bridge. They pace in charred suits,
the hands lift, point and ache and fly at sunset as cold dark
birds. They will hover over the dead ones: a family shattered
by military, buried by hunger, asleep now with the eyes burning
echoes calling *Joaquín, María, Andrea, Joaquín, Joaquín, Andrea,*

en exilio

From here we see them, we the ones from here, not there or across,
only here, without the bridge, without the arms as blue liquid
quenching the secret thirst of unmarked graves, without
our flesh journeying refuge or pilgrimage; not passengers
on imaginary ships sailing between reef and sky, we that die
here awake on Harrison Street, on Excelsior Avenue clutching
the tenderness of chrome radios, whispering to the saints
in supermarkets, motionless in the chasms of playgrounds,
searching at 9 a.m. from our third floor cells, bowing mute,
shoving the curtains with trembling speckled brown hands. Alone,
we look out to the wires, the summer, to the newspapers wound
in knots as matches for tenements. We that look out from
our miniature vestibules, peering out from our old clothes,
the father's well sewn plaid shirt pocket, an old woman's
oversized wool sweater peering out from the make-shift kitchen.
We peer out to the streets, to the parades, we the ones from here
not there or across, from here, only here. Where is our exile?
Who has taken it?

A POEM-REVIEW OF *THE ELEPHANT MAN*

There is no need to talk about the acting, notions of fine camera work;
none. The rest about plot, movement, drama; unnecessary, frivolous.
Definitely nothing about pity, nothing. It is a story about a person
that builds a castle, a delicate English church, intricately,
with the left hand, slowly, with a flesh of danger.

There is dark smoke in the lungs, foams, secrets, in the mind of J.X.
J.X. lives in tenements, in tents of winter fog. A loud steam of iron
pipes juts out of the city as torn hair in the dawn.

The city sweats.
A man with the chest torn open bleeds on a table. A doctor sews him.
Two men pull straps tied softly around the black boots. They pull,
the doctor cuts. It is a city of liquid. All eyes squint for daylight
in archways and stone alleys.

The eyes are wary. They are waiting in ragged coats, in particular
corners of suit pockets, by the golden pennies. Awake, all of them,
waiting to see J.X., the castle builder, the one with one artistic
hand left; the monk-poet.

J.X. stays alive somewhere in the heights of a building, resting.
It is a building for the delicate. Who granted J.X. permanent asylum
in this hospital? Was it the mayor, the queen, the princess?
Why the queen?

J.X. lies with the eyes fixed on a window, gazes; where are you
Juliet? Mother? Where in this city?

There is no romance in this movie. Eventhough Anne Bancroft calls J.X.
Romeo, eventhough Romeo dreams in the balcony, in the castle, in
the attic of hospital bars, in the cage of mandrills, eventhough
it is all a dream with the same chambers and walls; one window always,
one frame of sky oxygen always, eventhough the left hand is delicate,
at times artistic, there is no romance, only black liquids streaming
across pipes, backs, ships, trains, tarps, streets, and cheekbones.

Applause

There are no curtains. We enter theatres. We exit them, yet
we never leave. We go home to a hotel, a room, an oddly familiar place
and we wander, we limp, the spine bleeds profusely, we criss-cross
the floors, slowly, we come to a stop, at the highest point of the
journey, we will open the objects hidden in our purses, the folded
mementos kept in seclusion; leaning against a window pane, at night
we will begin to observe the black boxes where we keep the eye

4

of the relatives. They give us a herring-bone comb, a cigarette
holder, a miniature mirror. We will whisper "you are very kind."

We walk at intervals, the legs writing, scraping letters on cement.
No one reads our jagged poems, not the pimps, not the night watch-man,
the police, nor the nurse.

The story of J.X. lies alone on the surface of a street. The few
that can read, run in horror, or laugh, or pray.

BLACK TENOR ON POWELL STREET

Come now, come from where you have stayed in the earth.
—Tzotzil prayer for calling the soul.

I

Between the St. Francis and
the palms

in the center
between bent mute drivers
on the side

of the last cable car dreaming
to the sky

you sang
from the asphalt altar

in the noon of sirens
and statues

the finger canes of the unbelievers
stabbing the wings

zig-zag seagulls black
notes
from your throat

full of mad choir
spilling on rails
gliding somewhere

bleeding
with the arms thrown
open

reading sunday night riffs
from the Fillmore Gospel

in the Kaos of the silent
bodies rushing.

II

Will you run to the pier?
across Broadway to the sea?

will you leave
the skin torn soprano moon
as you fly?

to the deep green jazz
to the blood sax waves
to the coral tombs of space

will you search
among the pilgrimage
of elder reefs?

whispering
dreaming
pointing

against the city through the fog
your X silhouette

reaching for Malcolm
singing

singing
Malcolm's last Aria
screaming

Return.

CHILDREN OF SPACE

I

On Valencia Street the playground aches. Children float through parking lots
riddled with the screams of distant throats. Daughter-hands toss the toy
over the clouds; invisible. The mother in apartment G gazes, not inhaling.
The father coils the fingers around transparent shoulders in the air. Slowly,
they undress. Only the stains of the assassinations remain on their bodies.
They do not speak now. They cannot speak. Willingly, they have cut something
inside. Vowels bleed across the sheets.

II

They enter windows. They exit through small openings. Even their bones
are changing. Soon, they will be unable to walk. The two will end
in a stance, nude; one pressed against the toilet towel rack, the mirror
speckled with images of rapid hands wet. The other hits each fist against
the living room wall: please   me/leave   me.

III

In the sunlight the children rotate in soundless collisions, beyond the rented

    structures

        into an infinite system of undecipherable signs.

ATLANTA ROOMS

for Patty Lee Yarbro and Bob Levine

> *The universe quivers during a second of silence*
> *and sleep reclaims its rights.*
> —Robert Desnos

I

The miniature graves can be seen by anyone
anytime. The papers have reported the rapes
the assassination of children
faithfully

so we gaze
and we stop

a black woman sings, the phonograph spins
someone is absent.

We walk into an antique store: suits from the 50's
a white hat; most suitable for an alto sax player
a book by Sir Lubbock: *On Civilization*. We wander

into other rooms.
It is leaning awkwardly in the poetry section:
Jean-Paul Sartre's paperback, *Troubled Sleep*
I buy a postcard

Side 1. A figure embraces a banner against
   the breasts: *Suffrage for women*

everyone is reading
and it is cold.
Everyone is remembering.

II

It is impossible to conjure
the off-blue 1955 night jacket, the aboriginal
Australian wife-capture, a thin woman marching
in the early 1900's, somewhere.

I see storage rooms
only. Everywhere
the storage of flesh.

Blacks at Grady hospital falling wrapped in white sheets
heart failures in the emergency room waiting doubled over
a wheelchair. Blacks

grimacing, gesturing to the doctor about an opening
on the inside of the leg, the veins, the feet swollen
with hymns spilling and humming

chariots used to come many years ago
you can tell by the tracks engraved
in the front yards of the master's mansion
chariots must have come, you can see
narrow brick pathways winding to the back
yards, where terrible rooms of servants lie
awake below the trees, there a woodpecker
carves messages to the sky

sugar, alcohol and blood on the linoleum tile.

III

What is sleep?

Is it the winter in Atlanta, the huddling rust on the ground?
Vendors arranging apples and bananas outside Grady?
An explosion of dying arteries silhouetting the heavens?

Is it a hospital
where ancient angels are ushered from ambulances
singing of a southern terrain buried with memories?

Is it the earth sealing the riddles inside small fists
prematurely curling
into its belly of silent rooms?

THE WAITERS

I

Inside the solemn black vests
a fork circles
the red napkin

it cuts
neatly through the *serviette*

women
keep the membrane on the lap
below the belly

fondled in darkness
by fingers

men lure it around
the neck

knowing it will burst
the outer layer of its skin open

call the waiter for birth
where is the water?

call the waiter for sanctity
where is the bread?

II

The waiters are gazing through space
into infinities of whispering altars

lit candles
mirrored on knives

sinister edges of stars
falling into islands of flesh

call the waiter for sacrifice
where is the wine?

call the waiter for penance
where is the salt?

III

The waiters are standing alone
bleeding

the voice singing *a capella*
pure

the annunciation of the devil
outside

IV

Only one celebration flickers
in the faded yellow studios and flats

an infant crowned by aliens and exiles
a benediction
of aching hands and eyes in hunger

V

In the smoke of balconies
under pretense of a Bruce Lee movie
we count our numbers

adding
the howling images of chipped thorn
on the chest

a cheekbone
a thigh

the cross on the wrist burns
and the cloth binding the lips
is gone

cast out
we are opening our annointed jaws

YOUR NAME IS X

for Victor Martinez and Tina Alvarez Robles

x the man with the hands trembling
x the unknown echoes of the shadow
x the car flying through the windows
x the woman with bent fantasy jutting
x the falling crates packed with blood
x the romance doubled up against a light
x the suit worn across the sweat electric
x the embrace of night and only night
x the eyes smoldering through curtains
x the hair dripping memories
x the nude posing for death
x the neck twisting away from the lips
x the mute performance of sex burning
x the signal that quickens the burial
x the street connecting the final touch
x the blouse stained with confessions
x the room waiting inside the whispers
x the wave flourishing in cages
x the mineral with infinite heat
x the scream fusing through the bone
x the animal leash swollen with tears
x the music caught inside the walls
x the lover biting abstract flesh
x the accident quivering desire
x the poem written and erased forever
x the origin of your name

THE DREAMBOXER

His eyes, they slant in exotic ways.
—Therese Covarrubias

(He wakes up, rushes through clothes. He dresses. Leaving the apartment,
leaving the gallery of silent morning rituals, he will penetrate the city;
facing somewhere, some jovial coat, some nude statue, some quick mirage
of shuffling ankles. He will follow the daily exercise of his existence.)

With his hands
the soft
ends of imagination
cutting across
the other face
blood opens
its bell
the sun in the air
rings
through marrow
everywhere
through the fists
and the shoulders
of space.

They are watching
everyone
seated infinitely full
of eyes
wondering
of incest rounds
tossing each other
nude wanting
the grave childhood
of the tracking flesh
open.

They have paid
to see you
your gestures
your signals
how you attack the counterweight
with footwork
how you seek the wet pendulum
of skin.

(He walks toward her body: his church. The stained glass doors are open.
The guards by the holy steps give ointment and the men in procession
are dressing her, baptizing her forehead, drawing her belly tabernacle
criss-cross with tongue and fingernail. They burn boundaries across the
back, thighs, breasts and lips, leaving, perhaps, spaces of the forearms
and neck unmarked. The choir rises, solemn, in the dark boulevard.
The guards kneel, waiting, huddled, murmuring the new obligations . . .
he walks toward the candles in her eyes.)

I will dress you
in textiles and glass
under
an archway of light.

(The body is humming in the distance inside a square. Men-lovers are
leaving with amulets; the breast-forehead, *churchbell of the father,*
the rib-arm, *hovering wand of the son,* the pubis-knee, *bleeding stone
of the mate.* He runs for the body in the center. The shrine must exist.)

(And she spoke)

Am I the figurine
inside the black box?

who will be
the sparring trickster
the laced glove killer
against me?

(Inside the coliseum, we sit alone on platforms
we are clutching empty packages. Our heads form
rosaries whispering *we want the prize.* We dream
of a purse dipped in blood, we know, we bet:
we will win. The loser will be the woman painted
on the canvas, lying crucified by our fast craft,
our sacred hate.)

BROCHURE DAUGHTER

You are opening up a brochure
a nearby clinic distributes these, it has three graphics

1. A doctor presses the heartbeat of a two-year-old child,
the mother leans back, carrying her, holding the soft limbs
gently.

2. On the inside cover there is x, and in the center of the fold-out

3. An old man with his levis overalls. His arms propped
back, fingers whittling the chrome wheels. He dreams in a chair
quiet, unshaven, traveling alone. The dim shirt as an open V-neck
chalice, lifting a power of transparent skin. Smooth filaments
whirling, flickering, a seashore against the off-white plastic
curtains. You gaze at x. You gaze at a four year old, her eyes
in water, black figures escaping from the oval ocean, the burning
cliffs, waves, moon, the lips wet. Then the eyebrows as ships roam
destroyed. Two scattered oars floating, splintered, under the dark
light of sky, shattered night, of hair, wind. You gaze at x, the bent
arm. What is it reaching for? The cupped hand as a shell curved
scooping air? Sand? An invisible father's finger? The other palm
pulls a balloon. X sees. X pierces. X will never ask, who is that
man reading me? What hands touch my shoulders? Why is he so close?
Why doesn't he speak to me? Look at my balloon! I've drawn a face
on it. See, the eyes, the head, the lips.

An M.D. weighs x, he places her over the scales, a nurse
from the office will take a photograph of x. They will print
flyers announcing the new facility. The balloon slips
x catches. Suddenly, she feels something near, approaching, she lifts

her face, eyes up
waves.

AT THE EXODUS GYM/VALENCIA STREET

Jaime, lift weights. There is no suffering on earth, not even in rooms.
You can feel only metal, white, pure, aluminum, the leather cushions, the hips
churning against the bed structure, silver bricks pulling the legs forward
cartilages, sinews; the gelatin dies. The arm in the center of the mat
the arm, alone, hovering by the lights, the fist, the hard father's finger points
Jaime. The virgin on your arm glows, the gold designs on her veils flutter
sweat, Jaime, there is no moon in this sky, no crescent of light underneath
the Adidas, only a horizon of mirrors, a band of loyal torsos burning
flourescent, curling into tight caskets of membrane, breathing out the voiceless
kiss of pain, the handsome smoke of soldiers training, counting the shifts
of eyes, the enemies, practicing alien maneuvers, silently, glaring, bending
preparing for ambush, stalking in groups of three, registering blood, going fast

to scream forever

in war. Jaime

MODULE METROPOLIS: Documents

A. The Sentry's First Letter

Honorable Metropolitan Planarium Committee

Dear Sirs,

First of all, I would like to express my gratitude, again, for having been chosen as a Sentry for the Planarium. Although I have had this post for well over a decade, it is not until this last assignment that I have finally perceived what had remained a riddle all these years; the Master Plan is all clear to me now, at last.

At first, in the early years, I was motivated by a particular array of intuitions. I felt that at some future point I would find myself in a position where all the desires smoldering in the deepest regions of my being would suddenly, as if by decree, become realized. I went about fulfilling the small tasks given to me. The little assignments that other Sentries found unengaging, I treasured; they were key routes in my private quest. After several more years passed my intuitions became elusive, they atrophied and escaped me at every step. I began to abhor the daily patter of a Sentry's affairs. I began to grow suspicious of the plan for the Metropolis. At one point I dreamt of coming to the Planarium at night and planting J2-crystal explosives. A burning aura hovered over me. My zone-comrades were on the verge of uncovering my role as Sentry for the Planarium; they would murmur furtively to each other when I attended zone meetings. I did not feel at ease in my zone any longer, nor did I feel a strong sense of allegiance to the Planarium. I was about to request a permanent leave to another colony, even if I had to relinquish the privileges of Sentry Class status. It did not matter. When I received the last assignment the fever vanished. I remember it well. After I was briefed on its overall design, I knew what I had been waiting for. Everything changed. Forgive me, I do not wish to burden you with these personal declarations. I will petition for a Declarations Hearing, as customary, after the report has been qualified for passage into the Metropolitan Axis Files, where I shall exhibit additional details. Let me go on and present the matter at hand: The Metropolis Module Report for the current year.

Your suspicions were correct. There *has* been a rebellion in the Metropolis. The Planarium's orders, although carried out for a large span of time, are no longer being applied. I remember when the modules were first presented in the Metropolis; everyone marveled. Although, initially some of the zones held to their ways, little by little they accepted the modules and began to act accordingly. Everywhere, I would hear, "Before I was so alone, I didn't understand these things, now I am comforted," or "I am so glad to be a member of the Metropolis." I cannot understand why the modules have been rejected and cast away in such a violent manner. No one can argue convincingly against the scientific principles on which the modules are based. Throughout the course of my studies I have never encountered another formula as impermeable as that conceived by the Planarium. Perhaps, this is why various zones are still promoting modules originally assigned to them, undoubtedly. Why would a zone community discard a way of life as unique and gratifying as the one proposed by this Honorable Committee?

I must repeat, your suspicions are correct. There *has* been a rebellion in the Metropolis! Throughout the zone-system many regions have taken it upon themselves to devise their own modules! This is no secret in the Metropolis. On the contrary, they often celebrate their individual module formulas. They go about the Metropolis flaunting their elaborate displays, making a nuisance of themselves in the established quarters that remain. But, it is of no consequence. Yes, it gives me great pleasure to add that *all this does not matter!* Please forgive me if this sounds extreme or disrespectful at the outset. As the report will demonstrate, the rebellion against the Planarium was only a rehearsal for our benefit! The zones are now aiming at the real target: themselves. They are busy destroying each other. It appears that their modules lose systems-control in other zones. I have charted everything. It is indisputable. As it turns out, what at first was a rebellion against the Master Plan, now has become the strongest pillar in its architecture. Needless to say, I hope these findings meet all of the directives of the assignment and your generous approval.

I have divided the report into five chapters and have added a few notes at the end. In order to present before you the general case in the briefest format possible, I have singled out Zone X and Zone S as primary data and outstanding examples. Naturally, as a Sentry for the Planarium, I have a full manuscript on file. I await your word.

Again, thank you for your kindness.

—Sentry for the Planarium of the Metropolis

B. Fragment From the Rebellion

It is an island of jugular explosions. A womb
of faceless bees, an armless serum of chaos
spilling out

Pulling the magnetic pulp of stones and glass
the abandoned quartz knives of priests
from the world

Cut open
veins from zone dwellings, petals from boulevard
hair, torn, the midnight suits, acrylic lips
the eyebrow blades, neon tattoos destroyed
with fangs, flowers shriek in venom

Desire drills a sightless bouquet of red knots
curling city compounds of skin, cartridges
of nerves through the fingers and

incandescent backbones
the trapezius gone into liquid
into pulse only, shadow

Rhythm gliding
going over green fur, wounds, metal play cages
imaginations

Into a journey of unknown triangles or circles or
lines going up, a vapor, a dark swarm of spears.

C. Untitled Note Fragment

Is it possible to be anyone here?

V

The next morning the neighboring renters huddled. The speckled weeds remained scattered, some congealing, bending towards unidentifiable regions of the Metropolis.

Soon, the neighbors disappeared in the distance; their shoulders tilting at certain angles, their eyes fixed on the peculiar style of their paradise.

NOTE:

Unfortunately, I am not at liberty to go into more details. The leading subcommittee of my compound would destroy this account. Already, they have intercepted and retrieved some of the chapters and are announcing the material as an imaginary story: a series of poems. They are calling it *Module Metropolis*. Once it reaches other precincts the title may change, but undoubtedly it will bear the stamp of the principal officers (Please see enclosed envelope).

D. The Sentry's Last Letter

Honorable Metropolitan Planarium Committee

Dear Sirs,

I must confess, I have withheld a substantial portion of information from the report, deliberately. This is a personal declaration that will not need an official hearing, as it is customary in the Metropolis. I bid you to treat what I am about to disclose as a gift and not as the duty of a humble Sentry for the Planarium.

For years now, no one has resided in the Metropolis! The modules which the Planarium initially installed were immediately mutilated. They were far below the level of intelligence of the zone dwellers. Although, it must be admitted, a few struggled bitterly to rid themselves of the scientific impositions mandated by the Planarium I repeat, for years, ever since I began as a Sentry, no one resides in the Metropolis. It is abandoned. We have built a new orb elsewhere. From here we examine your behavior as you deliberate in the quarters and dormitories of the Planarium. It is all on our screens. I was the last agent making it possible to give you the daily impressions of our supposed existence in the Metropolis. Now, you will never truly know who we are.

Good Bye

LITERARY ASYLUMS

for Francisco X. Alarcón

WRITING

(Writing is richman's work, therefore richman's history. Lately, the unrich
are growing accustomed to the forbidden pleasures of writing.)

R-writers live in immense warehouses. There they write at ease; all quarters
are at their disposal, anytime. They will summon the workers, the maids.
They will call upon the ushers, the watchmen at the snap of a button, the tone
of a finger, a casual flutter of an eyebrow or even with a rhythmic twitch
of a torso. They are to be served with imagination, magazines, graphic suffering,
light-tables, ribbons, rare inks, tall quills. They can dictate, murmur, jump
glottal stops, gargle, spit, jam the jaw out, point with the cornea, pin down
figures with an opaque thin triangle of elbow for the ecstasy of a thought,
a fancy, a dream, a vision (especially a vision) for an ether, a helium space,
an infinite image of a new warehouse: a turquoise clinic spinning in the future
filled with flasks of dormant immortal replicas, unmixed serums and hexagons:
crystals awaiting a genealogy of R-words.

No one needs to hear the saga of the R-writer that rejects the kingdom,
that undergoes a series of initiations, that confesses and casts out
the jewels from the family's purse heralding verses from the colony of the beasts.
There is always an element of suspicion in the claims of all converts.
It is said that the beast obeys the master's wish. Even if we grant that animals
engage in rational deliberation, a beast must follow the command or meet its
death. Perhaps the beast can rehearse loyalty, disguise allegiance while conjuring
plans to overtake the household. Perhaps after the overthrow a celebration will
mark a new age.

Will they still obey an invisible voice? Will the creatures be able to pronounce
the new language?
What words? What signs? What writing?

Obviously, unrich writers are not animals, not reptiles. It does not matter.
They are prowling at the master's gate. Most are feasting, many have repainted
the walls, remodeled the furniture, provided extra exits, taken the mahogany
bedroom headboards out, shaken the ivory tusk carved woman away from the staircase
entrance, stripped the floors, thrown out the serfs (in most instances).
After changing their names they will gather in the same rectangles: the kitchen,
the family room, the porch, next to the vegetable gardens admiring native art.
Somewhere,

in one of the studios, tablets of the ancestors are being placed openly
over velvet cushions. There is quiet laughter amidst the ferns.

There are no audiences. No readers. An audience is an assumption, an image:
silent flesh block of absorbing membrane. An idea.

Faces have the same diameter of cells across the forehead. Everyone wears
shoes, socks, stockings, underwear, shirts, blouses, shoulder pads, cuffs,
brassieres, earrings, watches, zippers, buttons, wallets, hats, caps, scarfs,
lotions, spray, has 10 fingers, 1 hand folded over the husband's knee,
the wife's thigh, the child's neck sitting, the eyes sitting, sitting, the ears,
sitting, sitting the belly sitting, the sitting throat, open, listening across
the tiers, the warehouse, listening across the floors, wet, clean, listening
to the writer read, write, words, reading.

Another idea of audience: the conquered, the unkempt, the wounded, the forgotten,
the dreaming, spread over a mat, the boards under blue light, they lay over
assemblages of coats, razors. No sofas. They fall back, back to back.

Does it matter?
The idea of an audience, the idea itself cuts into all descriptions, tears into
all experience. The assumption of an audience: *they are listening*. That is it.
Who listens, if they cannot gain power, if they cannot prevent power from being
taken? There are only guards.

No one is talking about handcuffs, wardens, stripes, breaking rock with long
hammers. Remember? No one was talking about fangs, claws or foaming fur.
It is a simple angle. If you think there is an audience, you don't see guards,
the eyes tracking your lips, taking your oxygen away into a hearse, tearing
the spine, the skin, off, making splintered bone shoot out with veins as ribbons,
as petals for a funeral bouquet. The body lays cut behind camouflaged watchtowers.
nude. You don't see their lapels stained with fluids from your syllables.
You see an audience only. You don't listen to the iron gates closing, locking
slow around you at every vowel; only audience.

You are only reading.

BEING

Who wants air?
Explosions disturb the quiet talk in the garden, the dining room.
Gas jets of flesh perturb the remote chatter of assemblies in the south quarters.
At best, the galleries will stage a false burst of bodies from a cell; a delirium
of actors will escape from a grey frame of papier-mache.

The theatre of the unrich will emerge. Applause.

Who wants air?
Who will destroy?

Not hurt, not mutilate, not even assasinate, but, destroy.
Can individuals perform this maneuver? Must there be group consensus?
Has the world ever known destruction or only change?

We are busy at the museums. We are going over and over and over the archives of our own bandages. There are no R-writers. There are no unrich. Even guards really do not exist. There are only bleeding asylums for those that cannot breathe.

Outside beasts and jagged strokes of color blur.

POETIK

for Yvonne

each day I walk
exiled in my own country
—Miklos Rodnoti

It is easy to see the innocent wing
of the earth
clenching beneath the wondrous open sky
and curl into the smoke
of an unknown small-town thoroughfare.

My father Felipe is driving towards the liquid
tip at the end of the road; he turns
into an aging silhouette picking crops for winter.

At 83, he dies. He dies with diabetes and desire
crouched inside a cemetery, forever
in the star-studded refuge of all workers
and in the last raceway of exile
from my half-brothers and half-sisters
that never spoke to him and that I
have never known.

You see, everywhere a secret crucifix glows
crowning stolen territories.
Can you hear the locking
of miniature cells for the unholy?

At this very moment
are you listening?

There, in the most festive procession
among the escort of trumpets
in the bronze maze of a child's imagination
there, the most solitary woman
bowing, praying.

Who knows her?
Who has peered into her cold cupped hands?

She witnessed the clever ambush
against the bodies that gather memories
at every dusk.

She tasted this voluptuous ocean
and its embossed confessions of ruin.

In 1928 she raised a black guitar
like an omnipotent iron cross of song
her lips in the gesticulation of dream
an actress-singer swirling in the future;
how she will speak and reveal
and light up from the rising throne
in her heart.

But, my uncle tells her
"Maria, find other work, these things
are not suitable for women."

At times, I return
to my father's speckled brown hands
and I strum
my mother's half-lit soliloquies.

Now,
I am turning this arid landscape
fast. How it spins and pulsates
contracts and falls apart.

Gaze upon it, poets.

Toss the phosphorescent rings
from your mouth
into the abyss of this world.

Forget about poetic answers.

TRIPITAS

HOT LEFTY COURAGEOUSLY WANDERING INTO A
JALISCO TAQUERIA IN THE MISSION DISTRICT
LOOKING FOR A RESTROOM BUT FELL INTO AWE
AT THE SIGHT OF WHITE COW BRAIN TAQUITOS
ON THE GRILL AND BECAME IMMOBILIZED

Show him the way, please.

STYLY STELLA ATTEMPTS TO FLIRT WITH THE WORKING CLASS IN AN IN-COGNITO SET OF DESIGNER JEANS FRAMED BY UNSHAMPOOED HEAD AND BAGGY-SOCKED TRACK SHOES PLAID TOP (OF COURSE) WHILE REALLY LUSTING FOR BIG SCENES IN UP-TOWN SNAZZ

Tough life these days.

ENRIQUE CACIQUE PICKS UP THE LATEST NEWS
& BROODS ABOUT THE BEST POWER PLAY POSSIBLE
TONIGHT AT THE BARRIO MEETING IN ORDER TO
BRING ABOUT REAL CHANGE & ADD A LITTLE SPICY
SPACE TO THE NEIGHBORHOOD LIKE THE OLD DAYS

¡Que viva La Revolucion!

POLYESTER PAUL CALCULATING WHETHER OR NOT
TO JUMP INTO THE GAY/LESBIAN LIBERATION
DAY MARCH ON THE CORNER OF CASTRO & 18TH
OR WHETHER TO GO AHEAD AND LET GO AND
PURCHASE A TIGER PRINT SHIRT FOR HIMSELF
AFTER A COOL GIN & TONIC IN THE SLICK BAR
BEHIND HIM AND WAIT SUAVELY FOR THE NEXT
DEMONSTRATION

Poly, how about a wet cracker?

JUBILANT JEFFREY DOING THE BEST POSSIBLE
TO ATTAIN AN ACCURATE VERSION OF TRANS-
CENDANT SOUL THROUGH CORRESPONDENCE COURSES
IN A TOO-CLEAN ADMINISTRATIVE ASSISTANT'S
STUDIO TOWERING OVER THE SMOLDERING PHANTAS-
MAGORIC AND SWELLING CONGLOMERATE HEART OF
THE CITY

Pray hard, jack.

HEAVY POET AT THE MIKE CONCENTRATES
THROUGH HORN RIMMED GLASSES TAKING
DEEP CAMEL DRAGS COUGHING WITH AN
ACCENT OF HARD LIFE WEARING AN HONEST
CROSS-CULTURAL SAMPLE OF BUTTONS ON
THE VEST BOUGHT AT THRIFTOWN ON 16TH
& MISSION ST. CRACKS A MARLON BRANDO
GRIN AT A PERCEIVED GROUPIE AND PROCEEDS
TO DELIVER HEAVY TUNES IN STREET STAC-
CATO AT TIMES GRITTING THE UNFLOSSED
TEETH ROCKING BACK AND FORTH AGAINST
THE PODIUM WHILE BEING VIDEO-TAPED FOR
INTERNATIONAL DISSEMINATION TO THE MASSES

Applause.

ASPIRING ARNOLD ABSORBING A MIDDLE CLASS
COOLER IN THE LOUNGE OF UPWARD MOBILITY
STROKES HIS TIE BECAUSE HE DESERVES IT
AFTER ALL THE YEARS OF TUFF STRUGGLE IN
THE BOULEVARDS OF THIRD WORLD OPPRESSION
RHYTHMICALLY IDENTIFIES WITH THE *CORAZON*
CALCOS TRAMOS BAGGIES AND *TANDOS* OF ZESTY
ZOOT SUIT EFFERVESCENCE STRUTS DOWN HIS
OLD STOMPING GROUNDS SNAPPING HIS CHAIN
OH SO *BADLY*

Puro pedo.

TAB CAT HURDLING INTO CECILIA'S GARDEN
ACROSS THE STREET SNIFFING AT THE ORANGE
HONEY PETALED BURSTS IN THE ODD JUNGLE
CALMLY DESTROYS THE MENACING BUG CACKLING
OVER ITS HEAD CHEWS ON AND BOPS TO THE
MAGNOLIAS BEYOND

My hero on Capp Street.

PHOTO-POEM OF
THE CHICANO MORATORIUM
1980/L.A.

PHOTO-POEM OF THE CHICANO MORATORIUM 1980 / L.A.

Photo I. Pilgrimage

The march is holy. we are bleeding. the paper crosses unfold
after ten years. stretching out their arms. nailed. with spray
paint. into the breasts of the faithful. followers. they bleed
who we are. we carry the dead body. dragging it on asphalt
America. we raise our candle arms. our fingers are lit. in
celebration. illuminating. the dark dome of sky. over Whittier
Boulevard. below. there are no faces. only one. eye. opening its
lens. it. counts the merchants locking iron veils. silently
secretly. as we approach. their gold is hidden. they have
buried diamond sins in the refrigerators. under the blue
velvet sofas. they are guarding a vault. of uncut ring
fingers. the candles sweat. who tattooed the santo-man on our
forehead? Ruben Salazar. we touch the round wound with saliva
the clot of smoke. a decade of torn skin. trophies. medallions
of skull. spine. and soul. spilled. jammed. on the grass. gone
forever. beneath the moon-gray numbers of L.A.P.D. August 29
1970. running. searching for a piece. of open street. *paraíso
negro*. pleading to the tear-gas virgins. appearing over the
helmet horns of the swat-men. iridescent. we walk. floating
digging deep. passing Evergreen cemetery. passing the long
bone palms shooting green air. stars. as we count the death
stones. burning. white. rectangles. into our eyes. processions
have no gods. we know. they know. the witnesses. on the sidewalks
the thirty-two year old mother with three. children. no
husband. by the fire hydrant. the bakers. the mechanics leaning
on the fence. spinning box wrenches. in space. the grandfather
on the wheelchair saluting us. as we pass. as we chant. as we
scream. as we carry the cross. a park with vendors appears
ahead

Photo 2. Oasis/We Gather/Audience/Wide-Angle

We drink tropical waves.unknown lips of sun &
fragrant oils slip. down our backs. *nos reímos
camaradas*. we gather & we scope the elements
the cop helicopter will never invade our lake
it will never drink our perfume. today we make
this crazy speck of twin-blades blow. away. with
our eyes. la Kathy from East Los. el David &
his chavalo Noel.la Eva rapping with Cesar
el Bobby. Valentín & Francisco. we slap the air
hard. pulsating. opening the rock. around our
bodies. liquid. flesh. pouring. circling. entering
the grass.el saxofón blows hearts & lightning &
Felix sings quarter notes. *chale con el draft*
pulling at his chinese beard. el Aztleca talks
about the cultural center in San Diego. power
plays in the dance group. we pull at the grass
snipping stems. making incense for miniature
altars. who can fill the chasms in the corners
around the shoes? the black net stockings
silhouette cliffs & shifting gravel stains
the shirt-tails. a question mark of buttons
surrounds the waters.flashing against the flat
buildings. we gather. in the light

Photo 3. The Speakers

Fellini said only clowns know the truth. they smile
in torture. never speaking. although their sound
explodes and destroys. children appreciate them. naturally
children are their teachers. a good clown always
learns from the rhythms and the voiceless somersault
of a child. children are the first to experience disorder
joyfully. they attack madness with their round bellies.
pushing into its darkness. plucking its hairs. it tickles
them. they dream of being slayers of the monster. they
gather. they stand on a mound. imagining they can speak
to it. so. they mumble. swaying their wooden swords

Photo 4. Anna Maria Nieto-Gomez/On Stage/Alone

She said that the issues. the mind blades. the ones
that whirl. cut. out. a jagged distance. deeper into
Kaos. alive. between the man and the woman. the issues
that ten years. knives. ago were etched. written hard
through our lips. the issues have remained on silent
funeral ground. fading. into chambers. brief cases
pockets. notebooks. by the off & on bedroom light switch
inside the fiber of pillows. that men clutch. at night
crying. binding female mate. flesh. falling cuffed gnawing
sheets. in masks. they confess. the dream images. writhing
in laughter. slamming the small of the back. is this
nightmare. anna maria? or. is *La Familia* loved in chains
only? the issues remain & the wind howls

Photo 5. Sunset

People leave. slowly. taking their cameras. back
to Stockton. Colorado. back. to Fetterly Street
some. pick up the cans. the leaflets. crossed out
& filled in with addresses. the vendors close up
& pack into the vans. looking back. the fence
remains. bitten with rust. sharp coils. making a
crown out of iron y's and x's over the sun. some
of us go to the bar on the corner. we. leave slowly
with a few extra rolls of negatives. black & white
who got the viejito in his wheelchair? or the Varrios
Unidos group with the placas? shouting *what do you
want?* answering (the vato with the hoarse voice)
justice! when do you want it? now! the stage spins. out
acrylic mural images. la mujer. con un rifle. together
with a man. marching out of the plywood Emmanuel
Montoya painted. jumping high. into the wet grass.
doing steps of being shot. suddenly. opened up. by
the torque of bullets. a gas cartridge pierces
the belly of the woman. her imaginary rifle disappears
the police lifts his wooden pipe. strikes one. 2. three
4. five. 6. seven. 8. nine. ten. times. on her back. she falls
falls.falls.bleeding.her lips screaming through the tempest
don't leave

Photo 6. Night/Aftermath/The Mime at Figueroa St./Tri-X

for Adrian Vargas

The mime moves. lightly. he teaches us political ballet
step. by step. his eyes have bodies. that stretch. far
into the air. of Latin America. tiller-woman. tiller-
man. beneath the *patrón*. the military. *La Junta*
fevers in plantations. deliriums. in Haciendas. still
El Salvador. light bodies. explode in cathedrals
the yearning chests multiply. into honeycomb spilled
muscles. flayed. floating. caught in the bamboo
gyrations of his eyes. feather-weight tendons. shutter
as he snaps the head left. staring into the room
of people on chairs. lined up. against the off-white
wall stamped with photo 1. the march. photo 2. a woman
speaking. photo 3. leaders at the microphone. photo 4.
undercover agents. photo 5. people fleeing. cut. dying
in 1970. he stares. over the bannister. past our
shoulders. past. the gallery wall. seeing us. rumble
murmur. rumble. scream. pushing. we sweat. smoking
jive. with cans of alcohol. wet offerings. to unknown
deities. seeing the moist walls behind us. open
the single eye. pointing steady. shooting. across the
horizon moon swaying its tattooed flesh through
the city. compounds of swollen curtains. an apartment
with a hallway altar. a boy passes by the crucifix
bronze. body of Christ. guarding a bouquet of plastic
day-glow roses. a blue candle vase. tapping light
rhythms on the ceiling. whispering lips of smoke
at the. end. an opaque window. shut. closing out
the night of violent winds and soft movements.

MISSION STREET MANIFESTO

JAGGED ANISE

Jagged
anise cuts through chicken wire on Mission Street
somehow

the perfume continues to escape. It roams
emitting its vapor

writing its vengeance on walls
and in the air
even in daylight

it jackknifes across the boulevard
murdering
the tranquil zones of the district

no one suspects it
anise the powerless

huddled in yards
in the mix of its own liquor

tossing
its idea
into the random alleys

between
and in front of condemned apartments.

It is seeking everyone

police cannot throw a net or surround it
merchants cannot lock up and remain secure
nuns have accepted it under strict orders

who would imagine
that a peculiar caged breath
is slowly conquering the death of the city?

ARE YOU DOING THAT NEW AMERIKAN THING?

*for all movement, ex-movement and anti-movement affiliates and
for Brandi Treviño*

Are you doing that new Amerikan thing?
Sweet thing, handsome thing, that thing about coming out, all the way out
About telling her, her telling him, telling us, telling them that we
Must kill the revolutionary soul, because it was only a magical thing
A momentary thing, a thing outside of time, a sixties thing, a sacred thing
A brown beret thing, a grassroot thing, a loud thing, a spontaneous thing
A Viet Nam thing, a white radical thing, an Aztlan thing, a Cholo thing
A nationalist thing, a for Pochos only thing, a college thing, an August 29th 1970
Chicano Moratorium thing, an outdated thing, a primitive thing.

Sweet thing, handsome thing, that thing about coming out, all the way out
On a Communist scare thing, a Red thing, a let's go back to war thing
Because we must stop the El Salvador thing because it could lead to another
    Nicaragua
Thing because we need Reagun and Order in the Americas thing.

Are you doing that new Amerikan thing?

The chains, pins and leather thing
The aluminum thing
The transparent plastik underwear thing
The lonely boulevard thing
The hopeless existentialist thing
The neo-Paris melancholy thing
The nightmare thing
The urban artist thing
The laughing thing
The serious suicide thing
The New Amerikan Chicano thing
The end of the world thing
The victim thing
The enlightened quasi-political thing
The university hussle for the pie thing?
The *We Are the Community* thing

Are you doing that new Amerikan thing?

The *nacimos para morir* thing
The *yo te protejo* thing
The *Dios y Hombre* thing
The *quien sabe* thing
The *así nomás* thing
The *todo se acaba* thing
The *la vida es un misterio* thing
The *quisiera ser* thing
The *vato firme* thing
The *chavala de aquellas* thing
The *no me toques* thing
The *no quiero problemas* thing

Are you doing that new Amerikan thing?

Doing the be clean be seen by the right people thing
Doing the be macho again because women like it anyway thing
Doing the look out for number one because you tried the group thing thing
Doing the be submissive again because after all a woman needs a man thing
Doing the Army thing because it really pays more than hanging around the
    Barrio thing
Doing the women's draft thing because you can do it better than the men thing
Doing the purity thing because no one got to be president by eating greasy tacos
    thing
Doing the spa thing because there you will meet the right tall & dark & blond &
    tender thing
Doing the homophobic thing because you caught yourself lusting at an
    abberation thing

Are you doing that new Amerikan thing?

Sweet thing, handsome thing, that thing about coming out, all the way out
About telling her, her telling him, telling us, telling them that we
Must kill the revolutionary soul?

SEÑORITA *BLACK VELVET* LATINA:
On The Coronation of The Queen *

*The minute you are crowned, you become their property
and subject to whatever they tell you.*
—Miss U.S.A., 1973

Christ is a bottle of whiskey
with twelve pairs of legs sacrificial on high heels. At this moment
He is searching for a Queen among them.

No. Christ is Heublin Inc. Importer of a flask, a jar of women holding
their waist delicately, with one knee genuflecting over lipstick pools
of blood. No one knows this.

Because the staring men see:
It is time to elect the Queen. *Black Velvet* Dama. High priestess
of mascara and flesh on a throne of vapor, alcohol and hair spray
flayed before the male altar.

The long ties sweat. The shoulder padding pulls. The coordinator
of the contest lifts the microphone. His microphone. At the pulpit
it is His voice. His eyes. He lifts his microphone and points

To the product:

The iridescent smile
The maternal hand
The leaning and submissive chalice of the waist
The pious clavicles
The penitent eyebrows
The confessing hair

Paradise flows in her lips

She will take you to the sea. To the caverns. Tonight. *Esta Noche.* You
yes, you will hold her. Latin Mermaid in ice and desire. You will touch
her diamonds. Drink
             Drink
             Drink
             Woman
             Drink
Take my glass crystalline candle. Take it. Hold it. It will guide you
across the assassinations, the rapes, the destroyed arms, the burials
the nightmares, the tortures, drink, my mermaid. *Esta Noche*, you will be
a Queen. *La Reina para siempre.*

The Judges' votes are in:

Give her 5 X's for her thin hands
Give her 2 X's for her silent ankles
Give her 7 X's for her humble neck
Give her 6 X's for her serving back
Give her 8 X's for her nylon thighs
No.
Give her 9 X's for her nylon thighs
No.
Give her 8 X's for her nylon thighs
Yes.
Give her 4 X's for her nylon thighs
Give her 9 X's for her giving belly
Give her 10 X's for her Latina XXX

5
2
7
6
8
9
4
9
10
67 points. Votes. Coins. Drops. Bullets. Rapes. Guns. Braces. Deaths.
Coffins. Ropes. Chains. Wires. Wounds. Pins. Cages. Contracts. Locks.
Vaults. Keys. Knives. Tongues. Bottles. Sales. Labels. Belts. Lobbies.
Corporations. Drinks. Aperitifs. *Esta Noche*. Tonight.

Y Ahora

En este concurso para La Señorita *Black Velvet* Latina
de San José/San Francisco, aquí, señores y señoras,
este 22 de noviembre a las 7 horas de la noche, aquí,
en este Ballroom del lujoso Hotel Tropicana Twins
de San Francisco, se corona la ganadora de este gran
evento que ha despertado muchísima saliva en los círculos
sociales Latinoamericanos del Area de la Bahía, aquí
señores y señoras. esta noche, se corona La Reina,
Nuestra Reina, patrocinada por Heublin Inc. y todo
el espectáculo coordinado por la empresa CSI Advertising
Inc., sí , señores y señoras, esta noche de este bello
grupo de doce finalistas, se corona La Señorita *Black Velvet*
Latina quien recibirá los premios de mil dólares en
efectivo y un viaje para dos a la santísima ciudad de

Blackvelvet donde será reina para siempre, Dios se bajará
a tomarse unas copitas y ella, señores y señoras, por
dos semanas, será nuestra Reina.

Announcement

By law we must stipulate that Black Velvet whiskey is
an imported product of Heublin Inc. of Canada. We are
not responsible for the voluntary participation of latinas
in our campaign for profit based on the commercialization
of sexist images, nor are we liable for any party that may
take place in heaven and damages resulting thereof.

---

* Every year an extensive media campaign is launched in the Chicano Latino
communities of the Bay Area promoting the Black Velvet Whiskey Latina Queen
Contest (*El concurso de la Señorita Black Velvet Latina*). Several periodicals
publicize the event.

Translation of section in Spanish:

And now
in this contest for the Señorita *Black Velvet* Latina
of San José/San Francisco, here, ladies and gentlemen,
on the 22nd of November at 7 pm, here, in the Ballroom
of the luxurious Tropicana Twins hotel of San Francisco,
the winner of this great event that has awakened tremendous
saliva in the Latin American social circles of the Bay
Area will be crowned, here, ladies and gentlemen, tonight,
the Queen, Our Queen will come to light, sponsored by
Heublin Inc., yes, ladies and gentlemen, tonight, out of
this beautiful group of twelve finalists, the Señorita
Black Velvet Latina will be crownd and will receive
the prize of a thousand dollars in cash and a trip for
two to the holy city of *Blackvelvet* where she will be Queen
forever, God will descend for a couple of swigs and she,
ladies and gentlemen, for two weeks, shall be Our Queen.

ODE TO THE INDUSTRIAL VILLAGE OF THE WORLD

I

This is the ode to the industrial village of the world
Where the Third World dwells and works imprisoned and
Breathes in anguished rooms exporting a billion samples
Of dependence, depression and death to the sovereign
Kapital market of the singular and sacred and absolute

Empire of the World Bank

How long have we sailed and battled in this sinister ship?
How long have we been flayed over its corporate altars?
How long have we fed and hosted the invisible captain priest?

O village of streams, ponds, deltas, lakes, rivers and oceans
O village of deserts, mountains, jungles, islands and plains
O village of women, children, men, animals, fishes and birds
O village of Blacks, Indians, poor people, Latinos and Asians
O village of borders, colonies, barrios, cells and reservations
O village of miners, factory workers, process operators and slaves

How long have we been denied our name, our song, our power?
How long have we been buried in our own ashes, in our blood?
How long have we been kept alive in the pockets of the Master?

II

We have witnessed the Master's brothers cross the ocean for tribute
To the deepest auras of the earth where minerals gnarl and harden
All constellations and all the moist organisms of the world have seen
In Namibia, Africa, at Tsumeb, *Amax* crossing its arms to contemplate
At eight per cent of its import of arsenic crops throughout the world

In the village our lungs sprout cancer

In San Luis Potosí, Mexico, *Asarco* standing attentive curling its beard
Gazing at the new harvest of the colossal moaning arsenic smelters
Smelters of U.S. arsenic residues, smelters of high level arsenic ore

In the village our lungs sprout cancer

In Grafton, Australia, Mr. James Hardie, owner and illustrious King
of the Burylgil Asbestos Mine, wondering and pondering on the divine
Duration of the largest asbestos mine in the history of the continent

In the village our lungs sprout cancer

59

Asbestos in Brazil, Asbestos in Nigeria, Asbestos in the Philippines
Asbestos in Taiwan, Asbestos in Venezuela, Asbestos in Colombia
Asbestos in Korea, Asbestos in Jamaica, Asbestos in Guatemala
Asbestos in Tunisia, Asbestos in Sri Lanka, Asbestos in Malaysia

The Master says the Asbestos plant grows tallest in our village

45 miles North of Mexico City *Bayer* guards its robust affiliate factory
Projecting shares and dividends from the brilliant chrome fruit crops

          In the village our skin sheds ulcers

In South Africa *Union Carbide* and the *General Mining and Finance Corp.*

Celebrate the new ferrochrome plant in the Transvaal, a smelter to rival

          SOVIET CHROME

          In the village our skin sheds ulcers

In New Mexico, *Kerr-McGee Corporation* strips the land and computerizes
The offering of days and decades in the gross weight of uranium ore
To sanctify the nuclear future and illuminate a new age of intervention

          In the village our lungs sprout cancer

Uranium in Australia, Uranium in South Africa, Uranium in Texas
Uranium in Wyoming, Uranium in Canada, Uranium in Colorado

The Master says the Uranium plant grows sweetest in our village

O village of Mercury mines drowning the great Wabigoon River of Canada
O village of Mercury death flooding Bahia Cartagena waters of Colombia
O village of Petrochemical plants shrieking into the tropical night

          of Cubata, São Paolo

O village of petrochemical hysteria exploding into the soft and dark ears

          of Shukra El Kheima, Egypt

          Our nerves are disintegrating
          Our livestock is falling and dying
          Our children are born without hands
          Our children are born without bones

O village of chambers where winter is eternal and sunlight forbidden
in the Tin mines of Bolivia, in the Tin Mines of Australia and Nigeria

          The Master has given us seven long years to live

III

O Industrial village of the world lift up your green phosphorescent voice
Your jaguar throat, your tigress howl, your eagle chant, your condor words
Your leopard fists, your black bear jaws, your glistening whale skin shield
Your anaconda waves, your monsoon arms, your lightning fangs, your lava claws
Your hurricane mouth and storm from your deepest and darkest earthquake womb
And deliver the fatal strike into the billowing and bloodless global heart

Of the World Bank Master

Deliver the fatal strike to the export conduit in Third World nations
Deliver the fatal strike to the relocation of Capitalist industry
Deliver the fatal strike to the military ship of Imperialist cargo and prayer

And our village shall sprout a tender fire of invincible arms
And our village shall drink from an ocean of health and light
And our village shall weave the flowing petals of work without fear
And our village shall speak to the coming generations of liberation
And our village shall sing in harmony of our sovereign independence

NIGHTPAINTERS

The Dusk of *La Guardia Nacional* of El Salvador

1

They observe the wounds. Only observance is possible here
in this daylight. At night, they will refigure with the palette
of moonlight, with the turpentine of fever. The brown wound
jutting through the shirt, into the air, will become a circling
nipple at dusk. Jagged streaks across the neck under the black
musk of tropical rain will stream and descend as sweating leaves
across the round and hard canyons. The destroyed backbone, the leg
and its innumerable endings, the mother's belly scorned with bayonets
the child's arms singed in ambush: only ink tracings of the night
being etched on cold ground. They observe. They can no longer
remember. Only observance is possible. They have forgotten their
villages: *San Vicente, Aguilares, Sensuntepeque*. They want these
remembrances; one of them runs and embraces the others, he points
to the distant mountains behind them, his delicate hand hesitates
he is resolute; it is not his village, no more; it is a gallery
of night's work.

2

On the shirt pocket the stain is expanding, slowly, with every village
he passes. Perhaps, tonight, the stain will become a gold medal engraved
with the symbols of the father. They march and observe as they soften
a narrow pathway around the borders of the crop fields; caña shoots
above them, covering their eyes, their medals. They annoint the landscape
with their thin fingers, drawing in the twilight, over the roofs, here
at the mound, facing Las Cabañas, here at the corn harvest surrounding
Morazán. They follow these umber maps with boots and enter. You
can see them from the hills; the uniforms are too silent as they pause
on the side of the municipios.

3

Waiting perched on stones or trees or memories; from here they can see
the teams of bees close by, steadfast, pulling new phrases from yellow
petals, weaving messages with the last edges of daylight. The uniforms
twitch, tear. Their eyes have become as large as the face. The face is
one eye pointing heavy iron rifles, aiming. It is time to design the days
as wounds, to go into the houses and trembling tents and suddenly scatter
the tender chests of unnamed wood, the family letters moist with dreams

and summer, miniature altars guarding a shadow underneath the make-shift
bed, the boards, the green candle vase screaming with its tongue on fire
and through the curtain doors, the dark flight of shrapnel into flesh.
Again, to tear the flesh, the moaning flesh of the giantess' mouth opens
across the village with the abyss in every stone, calling out and echoing
in the black dome of burials growing over the earth.

4

The small band hovers over the body. They gaze at the pool of a bursting
wound, unaware that at morning this body will crush them, these little
soldiers see wounds only, their eyes have been condemned to remain open
forever. That is why at night they will retreat over the horizon and
turn back once again and again they will see their valley of wounds;
this ominous painting mounting over the gallery of mountains,
coming towards them.

WAR VOYEURS

for Clara Fraser

I do not understand why men make war.

Is it because artillery is the most stoic example
of what flesh can become?
Is it because the military plan is the final map
drawn by the wisest hunter?
Is it because the neutron ray is the invincible finger
no one will disobey?

or

Is it because the flood of blood is the proper penance
workers must pay for failing tribute at the prescribed
hour?

I do not understand why men make war.

Is it because when death is multiple and expanding, there
among the odd assemblages, arbitrary and unnamed, there
among the shrivelled mountains, distorted and hollow, there
among the liquid farms and cities, cold and sallow, there
among the splintered bones of children, women, men and cattle
there and only there, the eerie head of power is being born?

Is it because submission is the only gesture to be rehearsed
to be dressed, to be modelled, to be cast, to be chosen
in the one and only one drama to be staged in the theatre of
this world, where everyone must act with the backbone humbled
with the mascara of bondage, with the lipstick of slaves under
the light of gentle assassination with applause piercing the ground
forever?

or

Is it because war is the secret room of all things to be kept
sealed and contained, to be conquered and renamed *woman*
enclosed by an empire of walls, vaults, hinges and locks with
the hot key that men and only men must possess for an eternal
evening to visit and contemplate, to snap open a favorite window
and gaze at the calibrated murder as lovers of beauty?

MISSION STREET MANIFESTO

for all varrios

Blow out the jiving smoke the plastik mix the huddling straw of the dying mind
and rise sisters rise brothers and spill the song and sing the blood that calls
the heart the flesh that has the eyes and gnaws the chains and blow
and break through the fuse the military spell the dreams of foam
make the riff jump the jazz ignite the wheel burn the blade churn rise
and rise sisters rise brothers and spill the song and sing the blood that calls
the ancient drums the mineral fists the rattling bones of gold
on fire the lava flow the infinite stream the razor wave
through the helmet the holy gun the Junta the seething boot
shake it do the shing-a-ling the funky dog of sun and moon
pull out the diamonds from your soul the grip of light the stare of stars
rip the wires invade the air and twist the scales and tear the night
go whirling go singeing go shining go rumbling go rhyming
our handsome jaws of tender truth our shoulders of sweating keys
to crack the locks the vaults of hands the dome of tabernacle lies
and rise sisters rise brothers and spill the song and sing the blood that calls
out swing out the breathing drums the tumbling flutes the hungry strings
and spin a flash deep into the sorrow of the silent skull
the vanquished lips the conquered song the knot in the belly of earth
break out through the fenders the angel dust kiss the methodone rooms
go chanting libre chanting libre go chanting libre go
libre *La Mission* libre *El Salvador* libre *La Mujer*
the will of the worker now the destiny of children libre
blow out the jiving smoke the plastic mix the huddling straw of the dying mind
the patrolling gods the corporate saints the plutonium clouds
strike the right the new Right to crucify the right to decay
the triple K the burning cross the territorial rape game
and stop the neutron man the nuclear dream the assassination line
the alienation master the well groomed empire the death suit
and rise and rise libre libre and rise and rise and rise libre
and rise sisters rise brothers and spill the song and sing the blood that calls
blow out the jiving smoke the plastik mix the huddling straw of the dying mind
forever
forever
forever.